Balloons & Other Tunes

Carroll A. Rinehart • Julie Strand

MMB

MMB MUSIC, INC.

BALLOONS AND OTHER TUNES
Carroll Rinehart
Julie Strand

Cover Design: Lynne Condellone
Music Engraver and Typographer: Ephraim Hammett Jones, MusicScribe, New York, New York
Editor: Carl Simpson
First Printing: October, 1998
Printer: Patterson Printing, Inc., Benton Harbor, Michigan
PRINTED IN USA
ISBN: 1-58106-004-1

For further information, contact:

MMB Music, Inc.
Contemporary Arts Building
3526 Washington Avenue
Saint Louis, MO 63103-1019 USA

Phone: 314 531-9635; 800 543-3771 (USA/Canada)
Fax: 314 531-8384
E-mail: mmbmusic@mmbmusic.com
Website: www.mmbmusic.com

TABLE OF CONTENTS

ACKNOWLEDGMENTS

The authors wish to express their appreciation to the many children and teachers in the schools of Tucson, Arizona who have inspired the development of these songs. They were written to fulfill needs, specifically the need for songs and related material that build language facility, attend to topics of the child's world, and stimulate the imagination.

Important to the critiquing process were colleagues across the land who have made important suggestions. These special friends include Dr. Juanita Boggs Svendsen, Texas Lutheran College; Marilyn Rinehart; and Dr. Sally Monsour, Georgia State University, Atalanta, Georgia.

Special thanks to Kata Pettit, a precocious four year old, for her responses to the songs.

Carroll Rinehart
Julie Strand

The song "Who's Important?" is from the book *Who's Important?* by Julie Strand and Juanita Boggs, published by Collaborative Learning Systems, Route 3, Box 1650, San Antonio, TX 78218 and is used with the permission of the publishers.

The lyrics from the song "The Witch's Itch" are taken from the book *Sing a Song of Hallowe'en* by Julie Strand and Juanita Boggs, published by Collaborative Learning Systems. Used with the permission of the publishers.

"Lady Bug Grouchy" was inspired by reading Eric Carle's delightful story *The Grouchy Ladybug* published by Harper and Row, Inc.

SING YOUR WAY TO LEARNING

Introduction:

A song is a most enjoyable way for young children to become familiar with language patterns, to discover the rhythms of language and to learn to express themselves creatively by inventing new verses for the songs.

All of the songs in this collection are original and have grown from many years of working with young children. The topics have been chosen in response to the natural, growing curiosity that children have about the world in which they live. Individual subjects include animals and other living things, colors, careers, parades, instruments, mechanical things, about "me," and others just for fun.

The materials are provided to help young children:

1. Develop their singing and speaking voices.
2. Increase their ability to respond physically, to achieve physical coordination.
3. Use instruments and sounds to express and enhance their ideas.
4. Play with language as an expressive tool.
5. Connect the topics of the songs to the world in which they live.

Good songs are ageless. Many of these songs will appeal to audiences of many ages. It is important that young children develop their ability to learn through many ways. *Balloons and Other Tunes* can be an effective tool to learning at home and in school.

Guidelines for Using the Songs:

1. Young children need much repetition when learning. They acquire their knowledge gradually. Singing, as a part of language acquisition, provides a base for repetition of language patterns, and a response to the aesthetics of language that keeps interest high. Encourage children to sing often, in groups and alone.

2. Young children learn with their whole bodies. Movement is a natural part of their expression. They should be invited to freely interpret the music through creative movement. Throughout, they are asked to respond to the accents of the poetry and to the beat and pulse of the music.

3. Developing good listening skills are important to all phases of children's learning. Help to focus listening skills by differentiating high and low pitches, loud and soft, long and short and the timbres or "color" of the tones. Children who "hear" usually sing in tune. Children who do not sing in tune should be checked to determine their ability to aurally discriminate sounds. For some children there is a high correlation between their reading ability and their auditory development.

4. Children's language development can be greatly enhanced through the song experience. Word transformations or substitutions are an effective way of helping children to "play" with their language. Responding to the beat and pulse of music and then relating it to accents of poetry result in a growing awareness of the rhythms of language.

5. Children need to develop an active imagination with sounds. Exploring use of classroom percussion instruments while accompanying songs stimulates such imagination. Listening to the carefully orchestrated accompaniments to the songs encourages imagination. Both tuned and non-tuned instruments need to be a part of the children's exploration into musical ideas.

Keys Used In Teaching Suggestions:

 indicates movement activities, responding to beat and pulse, or free interpretation through movement.

 indicates non-pitched percussion instrument activities.

 indicates tuned instrument activities, Orff mallet instruments, handbells, resonator bells, and so on.

 indicates singing activities.

 indicates language related activities and other curricular activities.

 indicates visual arts activities.

Autoharp and Guitar Symbols:

Chord letters and Guitar chord tablatures are shown above the music score. Fingerings for the chords are shown at the bottom of each tablature. The symbol "X" indicates that the string should not be played.

Piano Introductions:

Introductions are given for many of the songs or are shown above a portion of the score to be used as an introduction.

Songs and Teaching Suggestions

Balloons

Teaching Suggestions

Secure and share together a copy of the book and/or film *The Red Balloon*.

Take students on an inner journey asking them to close their eyes and visualize what they would see if given a balloon large enough to carry them high above the city, beyond the clouds and on to the moon.

Discuss if anyone in the class has seen or ridden in a hot-air balloon. Speculate on how such balloons manage to stay afloat.

Create a dance that dramatizes the floating quality of the music and the words. Experiment with movements which are smooth, connected and legato in nature.

Substitute other words for the color of the balloon and the "floating." (gliding, drifting, soaring, speeding, sailing, etc.)

BALLOONS

Words: Julie Strand

Music: Carroll Rinehart

Smoothly (♩ = 72)

Sing me a tune of a yel-low bal-loon

3

2 What Goes With Peanut Butter?

Teaching Suggestions

 Tap out the beat of the music while listening to or singing the song. Tap it on the legs, the floor, top of the head, shoulders and so on.

 Make up new verses to extend the song.

WHAT GOES WITH PEANUT BUTTER?

Words: Julie Strand

Music: Carroll Rinehart

What goes with pea-nut but-ter when you've got some sand-wich bread? Now

jel - ly is ter-rif-ic but try o – ther stuff in-stead.

1. Pea-nut but-ter and jel - ly, _____
2. Pea-nut but-ter and bac-on, _____
3. Pea-nut but-ter and cac-tus, _____
4. Pea-nut but-ter and grass–hop–pers, _

Pea - nut but-ter and jam,   Pea - nut but-ter and hon-ey, ___   Pea - nut but-ter and ham!
Pea - nut but-ter and cheese,   Pea - nut but-ter and may-on-naise,   Pea - nut but-ter with bees.
Pea - nut but-ter and rocks,   Pea - nut but-ter and peb-bles ___   Pea   nut but-ter with socks.
Pea - nut but-ter and plants,   Pea - nut but-ter and wool- y worms, Pea - nut but-ter with ants.

3 There Was An Old Woman

Teaching Suggestions

Put the pulse of the music on the legs (patchen) or on other parts of the body:

$^6_8$ ♩. ♩.   ♩. ♩.

There | was an old wo-man who | lived in a shoe. Her |

(It is important to establish the feeling for the strong pulse to aid in later creative language expression.)

This lighthearted song was obviously motivated by the nursery rhyme of the same name. The nursery rhyme can be used as a story starter for individual stories:

> "There was an old woman who lived in a shoe.
> She had so many children she didn't know what to do.
> So she —

Make up new verses. For example:

> "There was an old woman who lived in a boat.
> She walked her fish and she swam with her goat.

6

THERE WAS AN OLD WOMAN

Words: Julie Strand

Music: Carroll Rinehart

1. There was an old wo-man who lived in a shoe. Her face was green and her hair was blue.
2. There was an old wo-man who lived in a hat. Her ears were skin-ny and her hair was fat.
3. There was an old wo-man who lived in a dish. who swam her dog and she walked her fish.
4. There was an old wo-man who lived in a can. She cooked with her plate and ate from her pan.

Where she is now, no-bod-y knows for she ne-ver tells an-y-one where she goes.

Zim Zam Zigglety

Teaching Suggestions

Respond to the beat of the music while listening to or singing the song. Tap the beat on the legs, shoulders, top of head and the floor.

Play the beat on percussion instruments. Choose a different instrument for each verse.

Play the 3–2–1 (mi–re–do) pattern of "turned into a fox" in the last measure of the D E F# resonator bells or Orff mallet instruments.

F#	F#	E	E	D
turned	in-	to	a	fox

Create new verses for the song. Name a place to "Put it" then have it turn into something that rhymes with the place. Example:

...And put it in the sea...
It turned into a bee.
Zim, zam, zigglety zee...

Additional verses: tray...jay; drawer...boar; can...fan; floor...door; stone...bone, and so on.

For the last verse:

So then I took the _____ and put it on my knee.
I sang to it and talked to it and counted one, two, three.
Zim, zam, zigglety zee, and it turned into me!

ZIM ZAM ZIGGLETY

Words: Julie Strand

Music: Carroll Rinehart

5 Ridiculous Rhymes

Teaching Suggestions

Make new rhymes making word substitutions:

> Rode an elephant upside down
> Upside down, upside down,
> Rode and elephant upside down.

Play patterns from the song on resonator bells or Orff instruments:

B♭	B♭	A	C	D	E	E	G	F
(Stick-	y	glue)	A	blue	gnu	had	the	flu

Make up new verses.

> A Red Fred went to bed,
> Stuck out his feet and covered his head...

> A Purple turtle, name of Myrtle,
> Got too fat and...

RIDICULOUS RHYMES

Words: Julie Strand

Music: Carroll Rinehart

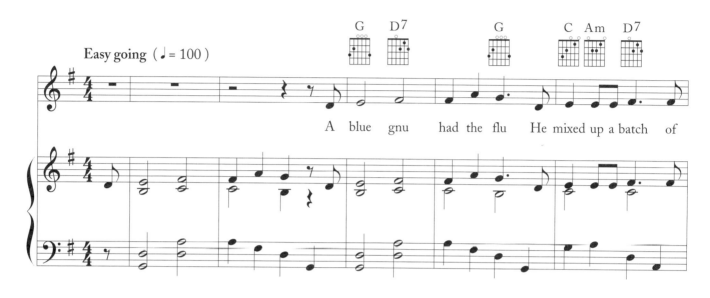

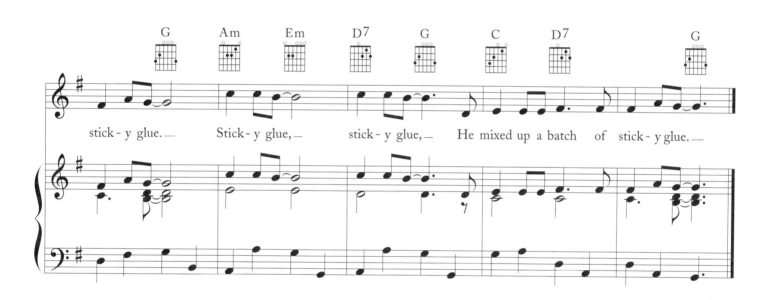

2. A yellow fellow, feeling mellow.
   He sat right down and ate some jello.
   Ate some jello, ate some jello,
   he sat right down and ate some jello.

3. A green queen was acting mean
   She jumped around on the washing machine.
   Washing machine, washing machine,
   she jumped around on the washing machine.

4. A brown clown wore a crown
   He rode an elephant into town.
   Into town, into town,
   he rode an elephant into town.

6 Colors For Sale

Teaching Suggestions

Respond to the beat while listening to or singing the song.

Play the pattern for "Colors for Sale" on the F and Bb bars or bells.

Bb	Bb	Bb	F
Col	-ors	for	sale

(Allow space for two bells between the F and Bb or remove other bars from the Orff instruments that the students may hear, see and kinesthetically feel the interval or skip.)

Find the "How much will you buy?" on the D and G bars or bells.

Make up new verses for the song. Name other colors. Find adjectives (describing words) which have the same beginning sound:

Red – raucous and racy red for sale.

Green – gabby and glorious green for sale

Black – bright and beautiful black for sale

Purple – pretty and proper purple for sale

COLORS FOR SALE

Words: Julie Strand

Music: Carroll Rinehart

With enthusiasm (♩ = 100)

Col- ors for sale! Col- ors for sale! Beau- ti- ful, bash- ful blue for sale.

How much will you buy? What shade will you try? Pay for the rain- bow and take home some sky.

7 Favorite Colors

Teaching Suggestions

Move to the beat of the music. Begin with tapping both hands on the legs. Later, make a sequence of beat patterns:

‖: tap   clap   tap   clap :‖   ‖: tap   clap   snap   clap :‖

Become familiar with the colors and color names. Make color cards for each color. Have students raise the color cards in the appropriate sequence to the text of the song.

Students might stand if they are wearing a color as that color is named in the song.

Play the "Is it red?" pattern (C C A) on the A and C resonator bells or Orff mallet instruments. (If using resonators, allow for the space of one bell between the A and the C bells that students might see, hear and kinesthetically feel the skip of the interval.) Place the A bell, lower in pitch, to the left of the C bell.

Play the pattern each time it is heard in the song: "Is it red?", "Is it brown?", "Is it black?"

Make up new color sequences. Substitute other colors for those named in the verses.

FAVORITE COLORS

Words & Music: Carroll Rinehart

14

8 Who's Important

Teaching Suggestions

Tap the beat on the legs, shoulders, and so on while listening to or singing the song. Later tap the pulse or strong accents (counts 1 and 3 in each measure) to feel the accents in the poetry.

Name other occupations to add verses to the song. Allow the students to experiment with the rhythmic flow of the language:

doctor
teacher
football player
basketball player

Find the following patterns on resonator bells or Orff mallet instruments.

"Who's important?"   F♯ A A F♯
"I'm important"   E A A E

Make a bulletin board of occupations.

a. Ask children to bring pictures of people in various kinds of work. Have them make up short stories of what the professions are and what the people do.

b. Have the children draw self-portraits of themselves in an occupation. Name their occupation and what they would be doing.

WHO'S IMPORTANT?

Words & Music: Julie Strand
Arrangement: Carroll Rinehart

Play the D Major scale to accompany the song.

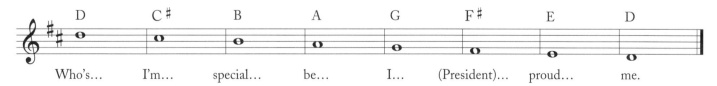

9 I Like to Pretend

Teaching Suggestions

 Respond to the pulse (strong beat) at the beginning of each measure while listening to or singing the song.

Dramatize the song, moving in an appropriate manner.

 Make up new verses. Name other animals and substitute other words to describe the movements or actions:

I like to pretend I'm a zebra
Watch me and you will see
I like to pretend I'm a zebra
Galloping and living so free.

I like to pretend I'm a turtle
Watch me and you can tell
I like to pretend I'm a turtle
Curled up inside my shell

I like to pretend I'm a lion…
Stalking and living so free.

I like to pretend I'm an eagle
Soaring and living so free.

…frog…jumping

…baboon…swinging

…hummingbird…darting

…puppy…barking

…little calf…chewing

I LIKE TO PRETEND

Words & Music: Julie Strand and Carroll Rinehart

18

you — will see. _____ I like to pre - tend I'm a but - ter - fly _____

flit - ting and liv - ing so free. _____ Pre - tend - ing, _____ pre - tend - ing _____

— I can be what I want — to be. _____ Pre - tend - ing, _____ pre -

tend - ing, _____ pre - tend - ing is just right for me. _____

10 What Do You Want to Be?

Teaching Suggestions

Respond to the pulse of the music (two per measure) by tapping the legs with the hands, tapping the top of the head, the shoulders and so on while listening to or singing the song.

Skip to the music. Associate the skipping pattern with word patterns such as "fly out in-to", "like to be a"

Choose a percussion instrument. Play the pulse on an instrument. Students might choose a different instrument for each career.

Create new verses naming careers and tasks.

> I'd like to be a fireman and put out all the fires
>
> …pilot…fly the great big planes
>
> …singer…sing a lot of songs
>
> …teacher…and teach each one to read
>
> ….fireman and put out all the fires.
>
> ….Singer and sing a lot of songs.

Play the mi–re–do or 3–2–1 pattern with the last four measures of the song on the D E F♯ bars or bells.

F♯	E	D
like to be an	as-tro-naut by and	by

WHAT DO YOU WANT TO BE?

Words & Music: Carroll Rinehart

11 Bought Me a Car

Teaching Suggestions

 Make a list of names of cars and extend the song by substituting new names. Do a similar activity with the animal version of the song.

 Play the "Bought me a Ford to drive to town" on the C and E bars or bells.

C	C	C	E	E	C	C	E
Bought	me	a	Ford	to	drive	to	town

Play the "Chevrolet in trade" pattern on the C D E F G bars or bells.

G	F	E	D	C
Chev-	ro-	let	in	trade

Using the same bars or bells play the "when the thing broke down."

 Build a response to the beat by tapping the beat on the legs, top of the head, shoulders, and so on.

 Make a new song by substituting animal names:

> Bought me a donkey to call my own
> He ate the sofa and the telephone
> Took him back and told what I paid
> They gave me a dinosaur in trade.
>
> Got me a dinosaur…little dove.
>
> Got me a dove…little deer.
>
> Got me a deer…little dog.
>
> Got me a dog…
> I took him back and he started to whine
> I guess you can't buy much for a dime.

Make the song a seasonal song:

> Bought me a ghost for Halloween
> He scared my mother and was very mean.
> I took him back and told what I paid
> They gave me (an ugly witch, a groaning ghoul, an old black cat) in trade.

Substitute other people (friends, father, brother, sister, grandpa, and so on) for the word "mother."

BOUGHT ME A CAR

Words & Music: Julie Strand
Arrangement: Carroll Rinehart

1. Bought me a Ford to drive to town. I just got start-ed when the thing broke down.
2. Got me a Chev-y to drive to town. I just got start-ed when the thing broke down.
3. Got me a Pon-tiac to drive to town. I just got start-ed when the thing broke down.
4. Got me a Cad-illac to drive to town. I just got start-ed when the thing broke down.

Took it back and told what I paid. They gave me a Chev-ro - let in trade.
Took it back and told what I paid. They gave me a Pon - ti - ac in trade.
Took it back and told what I paid. They gave me a Cad - il - lac in trade.
Took it back and start-ed to hol-ler. Guess you can't buy much for a dol-lar.

12 Buckle Up

Teachings Suggestions

 Respond to the beat while listening to or singing the song. Tap the beat on the legs, on the top of the head or other parts of the body.

 Play the beat on percussion instruments.

 Seat belts are one of many types of belts. Invite each child to bring a belt to school. The opportunities for comparing, contrasting and graphing are endless.

 Make up new verses by word substitution, changing "grandma's house" to:

"…We'll go to be at school
They'll be happy to see me.
Being at school
Is where I'd like to be.

We'll go to see the zoo
They'll be happy to see me
Being at the zoo
Is where I'd like to be.

BUCKLE UP

Words & Music: Carroll Rinehart

13 My Instruments

Respond to the beat of the music. Place the beat on the various parts of the body while listening to or singing the song.

Find ways of moving to "it plays fast" and "it plays slow" to demonstrate the contrast in duration and the fast-slow qualities.

Take each of the antonym pairs (fast-slow, high-low) and expand each term:

fast	faster	fastest
slow	slower	slowest
high	higher	highest
low	lower	lowest

Allow each student to select one of the three word groupings and develop individual sentence responses.

A propeller plane is fast.
A jet is faster.
A rocket is the fastest.
The 8 foot fence is high.
The 9 foot fence is higher.
The 10 foot fence is the highest.

Make up new verses about other instruments:
tiny wood block–tick-a-tock
saxophone   –all alone

(Some students may not be able to rhyme easily. In such cases simply repeat the "all alone.")

Experiment with the duration of sounds on percussion instruments. Choose an instrument with short sounds to play "it plays fast" and different percussion instrument with longer duration of sound to play "it plays slow."

Play the pattern "it plays high" on the F♯ and high B resonator bells or Orff bars. Play the pattern "It plays low" on the F♯ G A B resonators.

it	plays	high	it	plays	low
F♯	F♯	B	AG	F♯	E

26

MY INSTRUMENTS

Words: Julie Strand

Music: Carroll Rinehart

14 The Big Parade

Teaching Suggestions

Make a parade. Pretend to play various instruments. Decide how the hands would be placed when playing each of the instruments.

Identify the instruments by name from their pictures. (If possible have demonstrations of the instruments for the children.)

Make up new verses for other instruments:

…"Oh, I like to play on the triangle
Hear its ting, ting, tingy, ting, ting."

…"Oh, I like to play on the wooden sticks
Hear their click, click, clickety click-clicks."

Experiment with classroom percussion instruments. Find ways of playing them for a variety of sounds—loud, soft, fast, slow, etc.

Name the instrument from listening to the sound. (Play instruments behind a screen and ask children to name the instruments.)

THE BIG PARADE

Words & Music: Carroll Rinehart

28

The Circus Parade

Teaching Suggestions

 Show pictures of a circus and/or circus parade. Talk about the events that take place at a circus—the animals and the people who perform acts at the circus.

"What are the first three words that come to mind when you hear the word 'circus'?" Pose this question to students, giving no more than 30 seconds for them to respond individually on paper. Begin listing the selected words on the board, noting which words appear more than once. Create a bar or line graph to show the frequency of any words mentioned more than once or select in any other manner desired.

 Respond to the beat. Place the beat on various parts of the body while listening to or singing the song.

March to the beat, pretending to be the Circus Parade. Students might be members of the circus band, circus trainers, clowns and so on.

 Make up new verses listing animals or people in the parade.

THE CIRCUS PARADE

Words & Music: Carroll Rinehart

16 Baby Animals

Teaching Suggestions

 Make a list of names of baby animals: puppy, kitten, colt, calf, lamb and so on. Find a name with the same beginning sounds to make new verses.

 Create a free dance to the music. (Do not direct the style of movement, but allow for a free rhythmic response to the song.)

 Allow students the opportunity to experiment with the rhythm with a few percussion instruments. Listen for the percussion instruments in the recording and choose some with similar sounds.

 The first verse of this song has many words beginning with the letter "p". Students will have fun trying to recite a tongue twister which makes extensive use of words having an initial "p" sound.:

> Peter Piper picked a peck of pickled peppers. How many pecks of pickled peppers did Peter Piper pick?

Allow students to select any initial sound they wish and create tongue twisters of their own.

Find an animal name with the same beginning sound as each student in the classroom. Make up new verses with the names and the animals.

BABY ANIMALS

Words: Julie Strand

Music: Julie Strand and Carroll Rinehart

(optional interlude)

17 Katy-did

Teaching Suggestions

Move to the beat of the music. Place the beat on the legs, the top of the head or other parts of the body. Move to the pulse of the music (counts 1 and 3 of each measure.)

Play the 3–2–1 (mi–re–do) pattern in the last two measures on the resonator bells or Orff mallet instruments.

F#		F#	E	E	D
On-	ly	your-	self	to	blame.

Then play the elaboration of the pattern:

F#	F#	F#	E D	E	D

While the song lyrics ponder how Katy-did got its name, students will be even more interested in discussing why each of them was given his/her name. The inquiry can be developed into an interesting homework assignment whereby each student returns to school with a brief written explanation to be shared with the class. The information can later be edited and turned into a classroom book.

Make up other verses substituting names of other students for "Suzy", "Mary", "Sally", etc.

KATY-DID

Words: Julie Strand

Music: Carroll Rinehart

18 Animals On Parade

Teaching suggestions

Make up new rhymes for each verse:

Now there's two—wear green, wear blue

Now there's three—drink coffee, drink tea

Now there's four—eat less, eat more

Now there's five—like to walk, like to drive

Now there's six—have fleas, have ticks

Now there's seven—named Keith, named Kevin

Now there's eight—come early, come late

Now there's nine—feel awful, feel fine

Now there's ten—are women, are men

Respond to the beat of the music. Tap the beat on the legs, top of the head, shoulders, and so on. Move to the beat. Create a parade.

Play the beat on percussion instruments. Choose a different instrument for each verse.

Play patterns on the following bars or bells:

Animals parading	E _____	E	E _____	E	E __E	_____
Sing a song of animals	C _____	C	C _____	C	B _____A	G _____
Some are smart and	D_____	D_____		F_____	F _____	
Some are dumb	E_____	G _____	C _____			
First there's one	F _____	A _____	D _____			
Sing a song of animals	D _____	D	D _____	D	F _____F	F _____

36

ANIMALS ON PARADE

Words: Julie Strand

Music: Julie Strand and Carroll Rinehart

19 Tale of the Cat

Teaching Suggestions

 Respond to the beat of the music by slapping the legs, tapping the head while listening to or singing the song.

 Draw a picture of the cat with the fifteen tails.
Measure and make a tail ten feet long.

 This lyric is filled with words that have a homonym. How many can be found? Try this activity in groups of 3, assigning each member a specific task: 1) reporter; 2) dictionary user and; 3) reporter.

not –knot	all – awl	one – won
tail – tale	there – their	for – four
but – butt	two – to – too	through – threw
nose – knows	feet – feat…etc.	

TALE OF THE CAT

Words: Julie Strand

Music: Carroll Rinehart

38

that's not all — that there was wrong. — One tail was perched up - on his ear. — It made it hard — for
like him back. — I'd make him stay. — So if you see my cat with tails — Re - turn him to — me

him to hear. — One fuz - zy tail — came out of his nose, — An - oth - er ten came — out of his toes. —
through the mail. — He should-n't be — too hard — to spot, 'Cause he — me - ows — and

purrs a lot. — Now if you think — this tale — is true — I bet your brain — is made of glue. —

20 Close Your Eyes, Count Sheep

Teaching suggestions

 Move to the gentle rocking (pulse) of the music (counts 1 and 4 or two pulses per measure.) Pretend to be rocking a baby or some similar activity to dramatize the rocking movement.

 Play the octave "skip" of "large ones" (measure 9) on the C bars or bells. (Remove other bars or set out the resonator bells with space for six bells between the C octave pitches to allow students the opportunity to hear, see and kinesthetically respond to the octave pattern.)

```
  C    c
Large  ones
```

Play the descending stepwise pattern of "small ones" on the GAB bars or bells.

```
 B  A    G
Small  ones
```

 Counting sheep is often identified with going to sleep. Talk about other things that the students associate with going to sleep.

One sheep, two sheep, three sheep—How many other nouns can be found where the singular and plural take the same form? Allow students to use dictionaries and work in groups while pursuing this question or assign it as an open-ended homework assignment.

CLOSE YOUR EYES, COUNT SHEEP

Words & Music: Carroll Rinehart

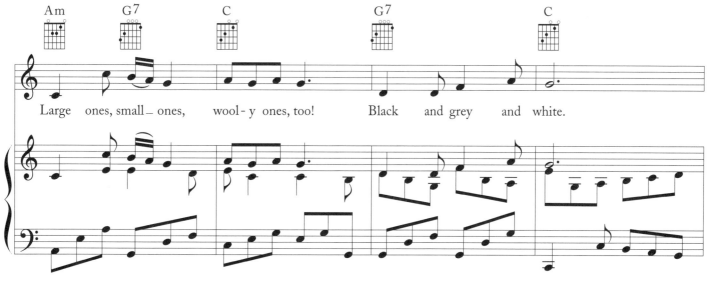

21 I'm Sick

Teaching Suggestions

 Talk about how the students feel when they are ill; how their voices sound when they have a bad cold.

Students may enjoy completing this sentence starter:

"I'm sick and tired of…" Individual responses can be illustrated and made into a class book.

 Move to the pulse or strong accents in the music while listening to or singing the song. Tap it on the legs, on the shoulders, top of the head and so on.

 Make up new verses. Substitute other words for "I can't walk down the hall." (Don't worry about rhyming. Explore the length of the lines and the natural accents of the words.)

Substitute words in the phrases beginning "I need _____."

Discover the "high-low" patterns of:

Oh, ick   (B–E)

I'm sick   (A–C)

cough and wheeze   (C–C–E)

sniffle and sneeze   (B–B–B–D)

Show the high-low pattern with Kodaly hand signs or moving the hand from high to low as the patterns are sung or heard. (Begin to associate the high-low pitch pattern with the mood of the song.)

I'M SICK

Words: Julie Strand

Music: Carroll Rinehart

42

sick, and it's no fun— at — all. I'll not pre-tend I'm real-ly ill, I

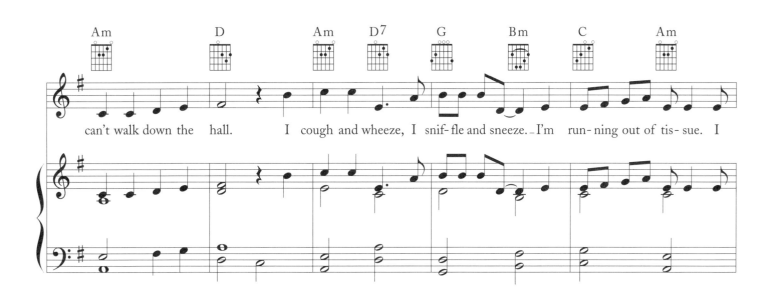

can't walk down the hall. I cough and wheeze, I snif-fle and sneeze. I'm run-ning out of tis-sue. I

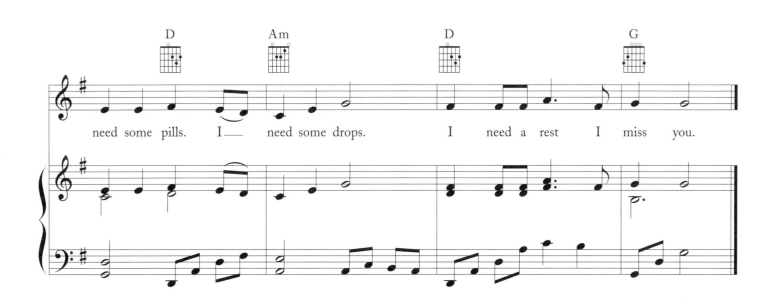

need some pills. I— need some drops. I need a rest I miss you.

22 Rockabye Robot

Teaching suggestions

Move to the beat of the music while listening to or singing the song. Tap the beat out on the legs, the top of the head, the shoulders and so on. Respond to the change in tempo, a slowing of the beat, in measure four of the song and then the return to the "a tempo."

Explore the "running down" feeling at the end of the phrase "The robot will stop" with a downward glissando, a sliding of the pitch along with the ritard, a slowing of the tempo.

Discuss how a mechanical toy works, the parts that make up the object and so on.

Make a list of tasks students would program into a robot if they were to have their own personal one.

A recent field of study is "robotics". Create a list of questions students would like to ask an expert in the field.

Allow those students who have robot-like toys to bring them to school. After examination of the various types, list those characteristics that are common to all of them.

Play the "Robot" pattern (measures 9–10) on the D and A bars or bells.

```
      D   A
      Ro- Bots

              B   B   B   F♯  F♯  B   B   B   F♯
      Play "Rock- a-  bye  ro- bot, In   the  toy shop"
```

(Be sure to allow space between the bells for two other bells that students may hear, see and kinesthetically respond to the skip or interval of a fourth. Place the larger, lower pitched bells to the left.)

ROCKABYE ROBOT

Words: Julie Strand

Music: Carroll Rinehart

Mechanically (♩ = 92)

23 If I Had A Robot

Teaching Suggestions

Respond to the beat of the music. Tap the beat on the legs or other parts of the body. Help students to feel the ritard (slowing down) of the beat to emphasize the word "wonderful" and then the very fast beat in the last measure.

Dramatize the song. Become a robot and move in a mechanical manner. Explore the slowing down on the word "wonderful" and then the sudden fast movement in the last measure. Find a way of ending the movement.

Talk about robots, what makes them move, how they move and so on. Show pictures of manufacturing plants where robots are used to do the work.

The following questions might be posed for individual consideration:

    If I had a million dollars, how would I spend them?
    If I had three wishes, what would they be?
    If I had my own jet plane for a day, where would I go?

IF I HAD A ROBOT

Words: Julie Strand

Music: Carroll Rinehart

The Three Toed Tree Toad

Teaching Suggestions

Move to the pulse of the music (counts one and three of each measure) while listening to or singing the song.

hold   the   **three**   toad

Tap the pulse on the legs, shoulders, top of the head and so on.

Find other words that rhyme with "fellow." Make new verses using the rhyming words: hello, mellow, etc.
"He never calls on the telephone, and never says a hello."

Look for pictures of a three-toed tree toad. Make your own drawing of the three-toed tree toad.

Do research: How many animals have three toes? How would you go about researching such a topic? What is the greatest number of toes found on any animal? How many questions can the students create that could be used in doing a class research project?

THE THREE TOED TREE TOAD

Words: Julie Strand

Music: Carroll Rinehart

25 Lady Bug Grouchy

Teaching Suggestions

Move to the beat while listening to or singing the song. Tap the top of the head, the shoulders or the legs. Then move to the strong accents (the pulse) of the music—counts one and three of each measure.

Extend the song by word transformation or substituting other names for "Sparrow."

yellow jacket	boa constrictor
stag beetle	hyena
praying mantis	gorilla
lobster	rhinoceros
skunk	elephant
dragon fly	whale

Count the number of syllables in each of the names. (Observe that rhinoceros has the accent on the second syllable.)

Choose a percussion instrument for each of the creatures named in the song. Accompany the phrase "'Let's fight', said the _____, 'Fight', said the _____." Choose one instrument to accompany the Lady Bugs response.

Play the melodic patterns of the following on the resonator bells or Orff mallet instruments:

"Waiting to pick a fight"	C D D F♯ G A B
"Fight', said a sparrow"	C C C A G F♯
then	B B B G F♯ E
"No', said the Lady Bug"	E E E E F♯ G

Discuss what makes students feel grouchy. Write individual stories using students' names in the title: "Grouchy Ted Goes to School," Grouchy Elizabeth Learns to Share," Grouchy Jack and the Sour Grapes."

LADYBUG GROUCHY

Words: Julie Strand

Music: Carroll Rinehart

With humor (♩ = 88)

50

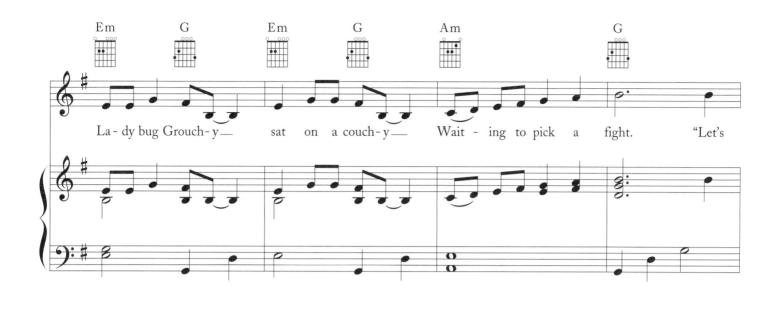

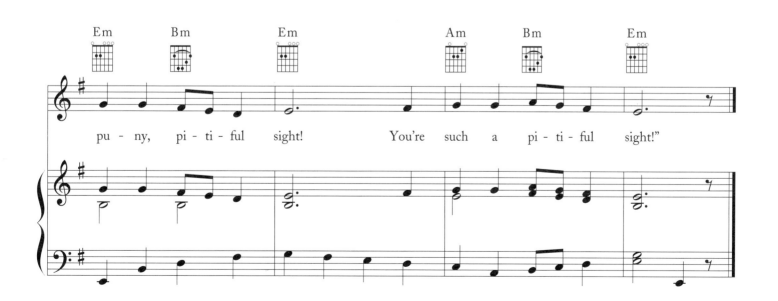

26 Dame Trot And Her Cat

Teaching suggestions

Find other words to use in the place of "Purr" in the last phrase.

Make a list of words in the song that rhyme with cat. Invite student to suggest other words that rhyme to add to the list.

Work in pairs to create a four line poem using the words. Make a melody for the poems.

Accompany the song with wood blocks or rhythm sticks to emphasize the short staccato quality of the melody.

Dame Trot and Her Cat

Words: Julie Strand

Music: Carroll Rinehart

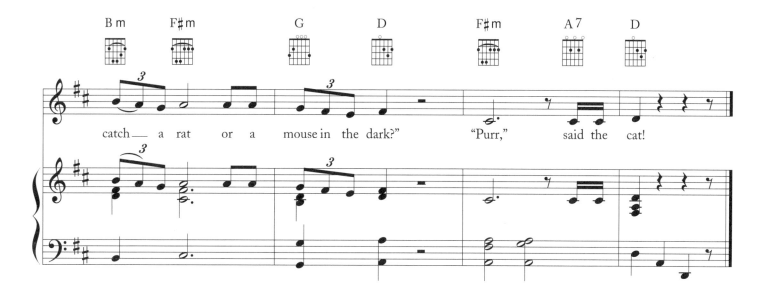

catch____ a   rat   or a   mouse in the dark?"   "Purr,"   said the cat!

 Dinosaur Dance

Teaching Suggestions

 Pretend to be a dinosaur. Dramatize the text of the song to direct attention to words such as thumping, bumping, and so on. Explore ways of contrasting words like roaring and creeping.

Respond to the beat of the music by tapping the legs with both hands to the beat. (♩ ♩ ♩ ♩)

Move in large slow steps to the pulse. (♩ ♩)

 Choose a percussion instrument sound for each of the gerund words (thumping, bumping, etc..) For example:

        thumping — small drum
        bumping — large drum
        grumping — guiro

 Play the instruments chosen on the designated words. Play the pattern "Dinosaurs" on the F and A resonators (F A) measures one, two, five and six.

Play the pattern for "thumping", "bumping", "stomping", "romping" on the C and G resonators or bars. (G____ C____) (When setting up the resonators allow a space for one bell between the F and A and three bells between the C and G bells that students may kinesthetically feel the interval.)

 Substitute other animal names for "dinosaur." Invite students to suggest alternatives and choose the appropriate "syllable column" in which to record it:

1 syllable	2 syllables	3 syllables	4 syllables	5 syllables
bulls	ti-gers	el-e-phants	al-li-ga-tor	hip-po-pot-a-mus

Discuss which names work best and why. (Both the number of syllables and the accented syllable make some more desirable than others.)

DINOSAUR DANCE

Words: Julie Strand

Music: Carroll Rinehart

Ponderously (♩ = 76)

1. Di-no-saurs thump-ing,   Di-no-saurs bump-ing,   Di-no-saurs grump-ing   Long a-go

2. Di-no-saurs fight-ing,   Di-no-saurs bit-ing,   Di-no-saurs light-ing   High and low.

Di-no-saurs stomp-ing,   Di-no-saurs chomp-ing,   Di-no-saurs romp-ing to and fro.

Di-no-saurs stum-bling,   Di-no-saurs mum-bling,   Di-no-saurs grum-bling watch them go

Di - no - saurs roar - ing, Di - no - saurs snor - ing, Di - no - saurs war - ring fast — and slow.

Di - no - saurs creep - ing, Di - no - saurs peep - ing, Di - no - saurs sleep - ing in a row.

very lightly

Long a - go they winked and blinked. Now they're gone. They're ex - tinct.

28 Dining With Dinosaurs

Teaching Suggestions

 Move to the beat of the music. Tap the legs with both hands to the quarter note pattern.

 Play the quarter note pattern on a percussion instrument.

 Play the pattern "end up being the feast" on the C D E resonator bells. (Be sure to set the C D E bells side by side with the "C" bell to the left.

$E^\flat$ $E^\flat$ D   D   D   C
end   up   be-   ing   the   feast

 Study pictures of triceratops and brontosaurus. Be able to pronounce the names and associate the name with the picture.

Discuss the concept of flesh eating (carnivore) and plant eating (herbivore) animals. Name other animals that are plant eaters or flesh eaters.

Compile a list of classroom or playground rules that begin with "Don't ever…" For each rule generated, develop a list of consequences. Allow students to use their creativity and have fun doing this exercise. Small groups might be formed, with each developing a set of rules for a different context.

DINING WITH DINOSAURS

Words: Julie Strand

Music: Carroll Rinehart

29 The Witch's Itch

Teaching Suggestions

 Respond to the beat while listening to or singing the song. Tap out the beat on the legs, top of the head, the shoulders and so on.

 Explore the difference in singing and speaking by saying the last two measures of each verse and singing the other parts of the song.

Extend the song by counting and changing the sequence of the numbers:

> Third little witch caught the second witch's itch
> on the tip of her third little toe…

> Fourth little witch caught the third witch's itch
> on the tip of her fourth little toe…

> *(Similar pattern for witches Five to Nine)*

> Tenth little witch caught the ninth witch's itch
> on the tip of her tenth little toe.
> She said, "It's a sweet itch, a treat for the feet itch.
> I'll keep it, I just love it so.
> Stay little itch! Stay with this little witch!

 Choose a different percussion instrument for each witch. Accompany the "Scram little itch, find another little witch" pattern with the percussion instrument.

scram lit-tle itch find an-oth-er lit-tle witch

or play the beat or simply use as sound effects as desired by the students.

 Wiggle, giggle and squiggle are words the children understand. But what about ziggle, miggle or biggle? Create a list of rhyming nonsense words and allow students to develop definitions of their own. Example:

ziggle – a disease that causes one to sneeze fifty times at precisely 9 A.M. every day.

THE WITCH'S ITCH

Words: Julie Strand

Music: Carroll Rinehart

1. First lit-tle witch had a ter-ri-ble itch — on the
2. Se-cond lit-tle witch caught the first wit-ch's itch — on the

tip of her first lit-tle toe.
tip of her se-cond lit-tle toe.

She star-ted to gig-gle, ——— to wig-gle and swig-gle and com-

man-ded the itch to go. Scram lit-tle itch, find an-oth-er lit-tle witch!

30 My Pet Pig

Teaching Suggestions

 Clap the pattern ♫ ♫ ♩ in the middle section of the song. Move in a way to show the longer duration of the half note (♩).

 Play the pattern on percussion instruments: rhythm sticks, wood blocks, drums for the four note short tones (♫ ♫) and a triangle or jingle bells on the half note. (♩). When students are familiar with the pattern they might tap the short tone on the tambourine and shake the tambourine on the long tone.

 Play the pattern "My pet pig" (measure one) on the G and C bars or resonators.

 Consider all the words beginning with "p" that could be used to describe a pig. For starters suggest: pretty pig; pink pig; pesky pig. Create a classroom book of pigs composed by class members.

Pair students and allow one minute for each team to generate as many words as they can that will rhyme with pig. Compile a classroom list and use it as a resource for writing simple poems: big; dig; fig; jig; mig; rig; swig; sprig; wig.

MY PET PIG

Words: Julie Strand

Music: Carroll Rinehart

60

hope he'll al-ways be   just a   lit-tle bit too wee   so he'll nev-er   ev-er___   be   sold.
hop-ing that he'll stay   just the way he   is   to-day   so he'll nev-er   ev-er___   be   sold.

Is-n't ver-y grand,   is-n't ver-y neat,   does not like to bathe   has four lit-tle feet.

poco rit.   *D.S. al Fine*

Is-n't ver-y huge,   Is-n't ver-y stout,   My   pet   pig   has the cut-est snout.

31 Peace

Teaching suggestions

This song is for the beauty of singing and to convey ideas about peace.

Talk about when individuals feel most peaceful, where they are when they feel peaceful, what occurs in their bodies when they are at peace. Discuss what is the opposites of peace and the "when", "where", and "what" questions.

PEACE

Words: Julie Strand

Music: Carroll Rinehart